LAKELAND HIGH FELLS EXPLORED

PETER WRIGHT

LAKESMAN
KENDAL

LAKELAND HIGH FELLS EXPLORED
Copyright © Peter Wright 2007

All Rights Reserved

No part of this book may be reproduced in any form, by photocopying or by any electronic or mechanical means, Including information storage or retrieval systems, without permission in writing from both the copyright owner and the publisher of this book.

ISBN 978 0 9555385 0 6

First Published 2007 by
Lakesman, 2 Maple Drive, Kendal, Cumbria LA9 5BN

Printed in Great Britain for Lakesman, Kendal

LAKELAND HIGH FELLS EXPLORED

Front cover illustration : Pillar summit

This book is dedicated to those fellow wanderers on the fells who shared with me the appreciation of a magical place ...The Lake District

CONTENTS

Introduction — page 1

1. Grasmere — page 3
2. Fairfield — page 7
3. Pike o' Blisco — page 11
4. Dale Head and Newlands — page 15
5. Kentmere — page 19
6. Skiddaw — page 23
7. Loughrigg — page 27
8. Steel Fell — page 31
9. Sergeant Man — page 33
10. Great Gable — page 35
11. Mosedale — page 39
12. Scafell Pike — page 43
13. Grisedale Pike — page 47
14. Binsey — page 51
15. Caw Fell — page 55

List of summits — page 58

Introduction

When I decided to write about my peregrinations in the Lake District I was well aware of the existing mass of literature about the area and wondered whether it was worth proceeding. That I did was only brought about because of my innate sense of humour and it is humour which figures largely throughout. It is therefore not a guide-book and is perhaps rather different from the norm but all the events actually happened. My only regret is that others now largely forgotten could have been included.

Although one half of my family hailed from the Cockermouth area my association with the Lake District was initially very tenuous. Visits in childhood were fleeting and my memories now are only very slight. When we moved to the Manchester area from the Wirral during the war, I was a very young child and not really aware of the Lake District in the ensuing years. Indeed there were other far more important issues in the post-war years. Pleasure was not a priority when times were hard. Also travel in the 1950s was far more difficult than nowadays. A trip to the Lakes would have been both difficult and relatively expensive and we did not possess transport.

And so it was that my walking experiences came rather later in life. Initial ventures were made into Cheshire particularly the area around Beeston and the sandstone ridge. Cheshire is not as flat as most people imagine! Following the enjoyable Sandstone and Gritstone trails, further trips were made into the White and Dark Peak areas of Derbyshire. These visits lasted for many years until the time came when new pastures were needed. What to do? Where to go? I had begun to hanker for a stiffer challenge and having subsequently passed the Lake District over many years on the A6 and then the M6, decided that it was time I ventured into **the** Mecca for fellwalkers.

Holidays were taken with my own family in the Lakes, but although I could appreciate all around me I spent much time contemplating the fells from afar; I was very much a tourist with a young family visiting all the usual spots such as Tarn Hows, Bowness, Windermere, Near Sawrey and other "attractions" of the time.

Personally I contemplated the fells wondering how to climb them; then Wainwright was discovered. The name Wainwright had begun to be heard in general walking chat but initially I knew nothing of him. Indeed my first acquaintance with his guidebooks was a rather disappointing business for me. I could not understand them, spending ages trying to sort out the structure of the pages. Consequently it was quite some time before their undoubted brilliance became apparent and they found their way into my library. Subsequently many hours were spent poring over sections that I would not visit for some years; actual fell-walks were always with the relevant book as an indispensable companion.

And so in this way I became a Lakes addict spending as much time as possible in the district. Nowadays I live there, having taken about 12 years to visit all the summits, some of them many times over. Most were visited before I lived there so those who make journeys to walk will well understand the time, effort and travel involved just to get to your start point for the day.

Those readers who are walkers will hopefully recognize much of the geography and maybe appreciate with a wry smile the events that transpired.

Nowadays my wandering is much more leisurely concentrating on those corners that I deliberately passed by in earlier years. Wherever I walk in the Lakes I never forget that the full and detailed appreciation of such a beautiful area would never have been achieved without the guidance of a certain gentleman from Blackburn named Alfred Wainwright.

1. *Grasmere*

Grasmere

Before any walking was undertaken in the Lakes, it was necessary to decide on a base to which we could return after each day's outing during holidays. After much consideration, it was decided that Grasmere would be the best option and what a good and happy decision that turned out to be. We chose accommodation adjacent to Parrock Green, which was to become our regular haunt for several years and where we spent any spare days that we could manage.

Initially we learnt that the owners were experienced walkers themselves so the business of drying wet clothing was accepted without question, always a matter much appreciated by the walking fraternity. Over time we became very familiar with the village and often found ourselves in Sam Read's bookshop usually hunting for maps or guidebooks. Being on a corner it was a magnet for tourists and occasionally interesting conversations were heard. Suffice to say two separate conversation end-pieces were the pick of the bunch. Firstly a broad Birmingham accent enquired: "Where's the beach?" whilst on another occasion the location of a famous mountain was sought by enquiring: "Where's Everest?"

A regular twice-yearly visitor always had the same room and even left his boots there, saying that he never walked anywhere but the Lakes so there was no point in taking them home!

Another time saw the arrival of a Japanese couple who were visiting the Lakes for the first time. The husband spoke impeccable English and we subsequently learnt that he was at Oxbridge. His wife became very concerned about the dirty washing and enquired of my wife: "What do you do about the laundry?" Without thinking she replied: "Oh, we just throw it in the case and take it home." The Japanese wife seemed extremely puzzled at this but did not make any further comment. Only later did my wife realise what she had implied and wondered whether the Japanese lady was in fact considering taking everything back to Japan, unwashed!

The self-same couple had seen notices regarding a sheepdog trial at Ings and asked what, in fact, a sheepdog trial was. I cannot possibly recount how we tried to describe the purpose and **modus operandi** of a sheepdog trial. Suffice to say we reduced things to their most basic i.e. a dog runs up a field to collect sheep and drive them through a series of gates back to its master.

"But why?" they asked. Good question. Efforts regarding practice, competition and exercise for working dogs were tried only to be met with uncomprehending stares. The matter was left in that they would go and see for themselves, no doubt thinking dark thoughts about the "mad English!"

Humour was always on the surface at our base, some of which was supplied unwittingly by the proprietor himself. At breakfast time the conversation always got around to the weather. Our host, whom we shall call John, was always consulted on this most important of issues. Invariably his was an optimistic note even when it was hammering down with rain outside. "Brighter later" ... "the rain won't last" ... "it often starts like this then turns into a fine day" ... "last week was a scorcher" ... "this rain is needed" ... etc. etc. The most difficult rite of passage for John was in 1985, when it started to rain in July, including Saint Swithin's day, and then rained every day until September, easily surpassing Saint Swithin's 40 days, the worst spell of wet weather I can recall in the Lakes. Even John, who had suffered this continuously, had become suicidal and was threatening to move to somewhere with more amenable weather. We of course only noticed the rain on holidays and other short visits. The relief was palpable when finally the weather pattern became more agreeable.

On another occasion at dinner one evening a general banter ensued with one of the waitresses on the topic of becks. To our shame we innocently asked if she could define what a beck was. The answer, loosely, was that a beck was a stream, which flowed downhill from the fells. Of course the opportunity then presented itself as to what, then, was a gill? Did the water flow **uphill** in a gill? The poor lass attempted an explanation but got nowhere and retired covered in confusion. All round fun without malice that typified the general ambience of the place.

Of all the scenarios at our base, perhaps the one that gave us the most satisfaction was that which involved an older couple. The wife was disabled and in a wheelchair. Her progress was either through self-propulsion using the hand wheels or with her husband pushing. One morning amid the usual banter at breakfast, whilst we were contemplating our visits to Fairfield, Sergeant Man, Helvellyn and the rest, we learnt that the husband and wife were going to attempt what for them would be a major expedition, the circuit of Grasmere Lake. Later we learnt that, like us, other guests had gone on their various outings and during the day had thought about them and wondered how they were fairing. When eventually we got back to base the excitement of the couple was very evident. They were very tired but had achieved their objective and had thoroughly enjoyed their experience, having **walked** part of the way. Our own and others' experiences were forgotten as we shared their obvious pleasure. They had achieved their "Everest" and we had learnt the importance of relativity.

Our old haunt is still there of course, but times and people have changed, as ever.

The memories, which have only been touched on here, will remain for a lifetime.

2. *Fairfield*

Fairfield and Grisedale Tarn from the lower slopes of Dollywaggon Pike

Grasmere, like Keswick and Ambleside, has long been a centre for fell-walkers. Thus it was one March weekend many years ago, that I found myself there with very mixed emotions.

The age-old problem of where to start caused much head scratching before the Fairfield Horseshoe was decided upon, if for no other reason than that it seemed to be the most popular and reasonably accessible route.

Two of us were to undertake the round, basing our walk on a book by Alfred Wainwright "A Pictorial Guide to the Lakeland Fells: The Eastern Fells." The full collection was to become indispensable after an initial period of unfamiliarity had been overcome. My companion left the trivial matter of the route to me, either through blind faith or, as I was to discover, a complete lack of comprehension where maps were concerned. The day dawned cold and bright as we made our way to Nab Scar, as I had decided to tackle the walk clockwise. Subsequent visits have convinced me that the opposite direction, from High Sweden Bridge to Fairfield itself, is a seemingly unending slog. My preference is to get the hard climbing out of the way early, so Nab Scar it was. Arrival at the top found two rather lathered and breathless individuals contemplating what lay ahead. We had not expected the initial climb to be **that** steep. Pressing on we arrived at Heron Pike, having recovered somewhat and been rewarded with tremendous views. By now we could see Great Rigg and Fairfield ahead, the latter being completely capped with snow; the whiteness being highlighted by the sky that was steadily darkening in the north. Our "gear", apart from reasonable boots, was not really up to the task, and although beginning to feel cold, we continued. Nothing, real or imagined, prepared us for the onslaught of the wind. This had been rising in strength almost unnoticed and now that we were on the exposed stretch towards Great Rigg and Fairfield we felt the icy blast of this unexpected adversary. This howling banshee of a wind was coming from the east and hit us with its full fury. Our clothing could not withstand this assault and the wind was going straight through us. We could not stand upright; in fact it was proving impossible to stand in any fashion. Any leg put forward was immediately blown to the west causing an enforced stumbling action resulting in no headway and frequent falls. It rapidly became obvious that we would very quickly have to assess our situation as we were getting colder, the wind not showing any sign of abating and the northern sky continuing to get darker. Usually inexperienced walkers press on regardless so our decision to abandon the walk was one that in retrospect was very wise, a lesson learnt early before stupidity claimed more victims. There is no doubt that had we attempted to progress further we would have got into serious difficulties being unprepared for such a situation. We retreated to Nab Scar to relatively calm conditions and then back to Rydal.

It has always proved difficult subsequently to convince others that I had once been blown off the Fairfield Horseshoe and forced to abandon a walk. I can only assume that these unbelievers only ever ventured onto Fairfield in fine conditions. I have since read a similar account by another walker, although I cannot remember whom, so at least I'm in good company. Maybe he was on the fell on the same day!

Fairfield has been walked many times since that first false start and the memory of it always returns whenever I visit.

214 Summits…
see pages 58 – 68 inc.

3. Pike O' Blisco.

Pike o' Blisco from Lang How

    A typical August day several years ago found me atop Pike o' Blisco in company with a middle-aged couple who apparently saw me as their salvation.

    The day had begun with a short stretch of road walking from the Old Dungeon Ghyll Hotel. I passed Wall End Farm and began to ascend very gradually the narrow motor road over to Little Langdale and Blea Tarn. At about 500ft. I left the road on one of the sharp bends, climbing in a southerly direction. The path seemed to have turned itself into a companion of Redacre Gill, following heavy overnight rain. Indeed it had seemed to do little else but rain that month. Those familiar with Lakeland will know exactly what I mean. To add to the fun, it began to rain again, the brief early morning respite being over. Out came the waterproofs, but of course our Augusts can be very humid, so before long the effort of slithering and splashing up the fellside meant that I was wet through with condensation. Being a spectacle-wearer, every pause saw the lenses steam up immediately. This, plus rain on the outside of the lenses, meant that my visibility was less than perfect, an understatement! The steepest part of this climb is between the 1,000ft. and 1,500ft. contours and at this juncture I was not sure whether or not I was enjoying myself. My feet felt distinctly damp and I began to curse the incessant rain. Eventually Kettle Crag lay behind me, and I headed westwards towards the summit.

However there was another obstacle to overcome before my goal was reached. At about 1,900ft. there is a barrier of rock which normally would be a simple scramble accomplished in a couple of minutes. This day found a miniature Niagara streaming off the rocks above me and I was therefore committed, however briefly, to some unexpected beck scrambling. Vibram soles and wet rock do not readily create friction, so a very ungainly upward progress ensued with oaths and expletives renting the air. This was very much out of character but at the time it seemed necessary in order to promote upward movement. The struggle had become personal and I found myself talking to the mountain, with thinly veiled abuse as to its ancestry. This can happen when you walk alone. Progress suddenly became easier with my eventual arrival in the trench between the north and south summit cairns. The main north cairn had long been an attraction for me, but sadly the once beautifully elegant structure had been reduced to a very forlorn heap of stones. This seemed to fit the time and mood of the day, as by now the cloud base had descended and I was alone on a very wet mountain top in thick mist.

I felt it was time to investigate the food rations and decided to find somewhere to sit near the north top. The rucksack was as wet as everything else and refused to co-operate with me. Simple knots would not budge, straps would not move in their guides. Even the zips on the side pockets turned against me with the sack material becoming jammed in the zipper. This was too much. I decided that forced entry was necessary and a little brute force found me inside the sack. Visions of culinary delights were rampant, but again the day's pattern was not to be overcome. Everything within was also sodden, as I had forgotten to put the contents into a bin bag to keep them dry. This was obviously a day when I should have stayed in bed. Eventually I was able to extricate and eat a very soggy sandwich to be followed by a much-needed cup of coffee. The pattern continued. The flask top had not been screwed down tightly enough and had been adding its contents to the general wetness of the rucksack. To make matters worse, the milk had separated leaving a disgusting slimy mess at the top. Usually, such minor problems were taken in my stride, but this series of silly events plus the weather had contrived to put me in a rather cross frame of mind. As I was just about to consume what remained of the coffee, without any of my usual relish, I was extremely startled to hear a voice, as I had thought myself to be completely alone.

"Do you know the way down?" I peered round and saw a middle-aged man moving rapidly towards me. I groaned. This was too much. I stared at him. He was clutching what appeared to be a "motorist's walks" book. "I think we have to turn left," he said.

"Left?" I queried, confused.

"Yes, it says so here, look", pointing to the book. I realized if I did so I was well and truly drawn into his problem.

At that point I saw another shape just visible in the murk.

"My wife," he explained. She seemed to be rather fed up; very wet, wishing she was elsewhere, hoping her hero would solve their problem. I wondered how two obviously inexperienced folk came to find themselves on top of a mountain in thick mist without map or compass, clutching a book of "motorist's walks". I decided that they must have parked at the Three Shires Stone and taken the easy wander to Red Tarn, taking the path up Pike o' Blisco from there.

"Where have you come from?" I asked.

"That way," he said, gesturing vaguely behind him, "we've got to get down". It then dawned on me that he, if not both of them, was on the verge of panic.

"We want to go that way," he said, pointing generally into the murk, "it says so here, look…" The situation called for a firm hand. I thought of his wife when he asked: "What's it like?" after I had briefly described my own route to the summit.

"Not bad", I lied, "a bit slippery here and there, a little rock scramble and you're on your way down Redacre Gill towards the Little Langdale road". The miniature Niagara I encountered on the way up was vividly recalled.

"How about you?" I enquired.

"Tough, really bad" he said.

"Really?" I said, somewhat mystified.

"Yes, it's very difficult" he said.

Suggesting that he ignore the instruction in his book to "turn left", I gave him as much straightforward information as I could and wished them both a pleasant walk. I then headed southwest down towards Red Tarn. It was very wet but not unduly difficult. I thought of my recent conversation at the summit. If my erstwhile companion thought that this was difficult, what on earth would he make of the route upon which both he and his wife were now embarked? He must have been feeling that it was impossible! Presumably I was being roundly cursed. I often wonder how long it took them to get down the mini-Niagara. Perhaps their book told them to "turn right" when they reached the road, to take them via Blea Tarn to Wrynose and the Three Shires Stone. I imagine the hapless husband suffered his wife's wrath that evening.

I arrived at Red Tarn in quick time, by then being out of the dense mist. A short diversion to the top of Cold Pike preceded my eventual descent via Browney Gill to Oxendale and Stool End.

Driving away from the Old Dungeon Ghyll car park I saw a middle-aged couple clutching what appeared to be a book of "motorist's walks" … but then I suppose the climb up Browney Gill is rather more strenuous than the stroll from the Three Shires Stone!

Presumably they must have turned left after all!

Whenever I see Pike o' Blisco I am reminded of this cameo, which always produces a wry smile.

4. Dale Head and Newlands

Newlands from Dale Head

Probably one of **the** most enjoyable days on the fells occurred one glorious August day in the late 1980s when I arrived at Little Town. Anticipation was intense as I had been reading of Wainwright's "Sweet Arcadia" for years and at last I was about to sample its delights. Indeed it is one of the many pleasures of fell-walking that many enjoyable hours can be spent poring over maps planning the next sojourn. I was also a little apprehensive, knowing that about half way round there would be a considerable loss of height, which I always begrudge, coming off High Spy and ascending Dale Head. I hoped that sufficient energy would remain so that the Hindscarth ridge could be attained.

As always in new territory it took a while to become orientated but soon I was climbing towards Hause Gate, being wary of the many shafts in the area of the Yewthwaite Mine passed **en route**. Arrival at the col signified the real start of the walk and Maiden Moor was easily reached when a quick visit to Bull Crag was made but the stop was very short as there was much yet to do. High Stile yielded a superb summit cairn and I have never ceased to be amazed at the effort put into the construction of many of the cairns in Lakeland. There are far too many useless and frivolous constructions around but the real craftsman-constructed cairns are, to me, a source of wonder.

A look around the summit plateau included a stroll to Blea Crag before continuing on the now steady descent towards Dale Head Tarn. Arrival at the tarn area revealed that one of my pet hates was before me, namely ground with little rocky knolls and depressions similar to that found at Silver How above Grasmere, which in mist is very frustrating and tiring unless you know **exactly** where you are. Today however was cloudless but bypassing the tarn on a pathless line took me eventually through a marshy section to arrive at the foot of the climb to Dale Head. I had decided to use the path from Honister rather than attack Dale Head directly from the tarn. This was purely for the reason mentioned earlier, to preserve stamina, and I was glad I made this decision for by now the heat of the day was at its highest and I was climbing for the second time.

By now the effort was taking its toll, for frequent stops were being made to admire the scenery, although when being passed by the fresh legs of those ascending from Honister, appearances had to be maintained and no stopping permitted, at least until they were further ahead! Eventually however, the ground evened out and the summit was reached. What a splendid, crowning moment! The **pièce de resistance**! The view from the cairn is absolutely breathtaking and I was grateful that the weather had been kind. It was only then that Eel Crags became apparent below High Spy, looking like a massive black wall. The Newlands Valley was in a picture frame comprising both flanks of the horseshoe with Skiddaw as the backdrop. To complete the moment, the summit cairn was in good repair; what a splendid location it occupies.

After a suitable rest to admire the view, it was time to move on. Exhilaration being high, I had wild ideas of going on to Robinson, but eventually reason prevailed and I made my way towards Hindscarth on a delightful path that enabled me to view Buttermere. The legs were now aching a little and Hindscarth's summit a mile later was welcomed. It would now be downhill all the way!

Here I was passed by two walkers going in the opposite direction who were heavily engrossed in discussing Moses Rigg, and his "trod" across to Great Gable and Wasdale from Honister/Fleetwith Pike. We see his smuggling now in a romantic light but in those hard, tough days it must have been an occupation fraught with risk, unless this is all pure fiction, as Symonds believes. There now followed a superb descent towards Scope End along a rather narrow winding path through the heather, which was showing it's full splendour in the sunlight. With both peace and solitude I was indeed in "Sweet Arcadia".

All too soon I arrived at Scope End having passed the Goldscope Mine. Unlike Coniston, with its highly visible scars of past mining, it is hard to visualize activity on such a scale in Newlands, but in the 16th century mining took place here in earnest after the efforts of earlier centuries proved unproductive, and was to continue for three hundred years. After the Company of Mines Royal had been established in the mid-16th century, several hundred miners from Germany arrived to apply their expertise in the extraction of lead, copper, gold and silver. How pleasant it is that the valley has recovered to such an extent that Wainwright referred to it as a "Sweet Arcadia".

Further descent to the farm at Low Snab was to reveal unsuspected treasures. Refreshments were available and I was invited into the kitchen to select my choice of cake all of which was newly baked. Two squares of delicious fruit loaf and two cups of coffee were consumed outside with a grand view of the valley. Much of the cake did however end up in the stomach of a very attentive sheepdog that never took his eyes off me all the time I was eating but slunk off the instant he realized all was gone! In such situations food and drink taste wonderful, especially after hours of toil.

Eventually it was time to go and a short stroll led me to Newlands Church. Surely this must be the most peaceful and secluded church in Lakeland? The church at Wasdale Head, St.Olaf's, is also splendidly located as is Martindale Old Church, but for me it's Newlands. A wander over the bridge and a brief stretch of tarmac brought me back to Little Town.

I had seen very few people all day and as I was walking alone this only served to heighten the experience of a wonderful expedition, which had been full of charm, peace, solitude and beauty.

If ever there was a need to extol the virtues of lone walking then this day surely had done just that.

5. Kentmere

Yoke, Ill Bell and Froswick from Caudale Moor

When I first visited the beautiful valley of Kentmere it was relatively little known. Indeed when mentioned in conversation with casual visitors to the Lake District the usual response was one of indifference born of ignorance. It was as though I should be pitied for not spending my time in the Langdales, Keswick or Bowness. Why spend time in this unknown, therefore perceived as less attractive, place called Kentmere? When I explained that for me the main attraction was the lack of facilities, thus a lack of tourists in search of souvenirs, coupled with a wonderful sense of space and freedom, then to some I was to be pitied!

Of numerous visits to Kentmere and **environs** the most vivid was that in 1985. Before coming to live in Lakeland I had read "Fellwalking with Wainwright" and was very keen to undertake the Kentmere round. Thus the beginning of June found me heading up the

M6, subsequently arriving at the church early, so early in fact that there was not another vehicle in sight. Not so nowadays!

Heading out towards the Garburn Pass I could feel the heat of the sun on my back even at that early hour. I wryly observed to myself that the day was going to be a hot one. Already I was heating up and sweating and it was only 7.40 a.m. I wondered whether I would see an adder basking in the sun on a rock as had Alfred Wainwright on one of his walks. Turning north onto the Ill Bell ridge brought a little relief from the sun and steady uninterrupted walking saw me onto Yoke and then Ill Bell itself in reasonable time. Yoke would only reveal the impressive Rainsborrow Crag to me when I was on the return leg of the horseshoe.

I was not in any hurry as it was my intention to enjoy what was obviously going to be a very fine day. Having examined the splendid cairns on the summit of Ill Bell, I was then able to contemplate the northern prospect of Froswick and Thornthwaite Crag, the latter seemingly a very long way off with its striking obelisk standing proud and dominant. By now the sun was becoming just a little too warm for comfort. Froswick was reached easily and the long gradual climb to Thornthwaite commenced. The track down Scots Rake to Troutbeck having been passed, my focus was entirely on the obelisk. It did not appear to be getting any nearer, but after a seemingly overlong trek uphill from Froswick, the splendid top was reached.

A short break to enjoy the vista of Kentmere and the opportunity to inspect the obelisk at close quarters, marvelling at the skill of the craftsmen who built it, was followed by the intriguing task of trying to locate the source of the river Kent. Having seen the river race through Kendal, particularly in the winter, it seemed hardly credible that the insignificant spring underfoot became the raging river Kent a few short miles away.

There was no doubt now but that the day was becoming extremely hot. Should I include High Street in the round, as was my original intention? A quick inspection of the fluid stocks ruled this out. I would include it in a future round from Hayeswater when Kidsty Pike and High Raise were my objectives. Quickly moving from the source of the Kent to Mardale Ill Bell, I then proceeded from the summit down the winding track to the col on the Garburn Pass. Before me lay a climb of a further 500ft. to the summit of Harter Fell.

By this time I had begun to experience cramp in my legs, and the prospect of the climb up Harter lay before me. What should have been a fairly easy climb became a rather laboured affair, taking longer than expected. Eventual arrival at the top found me very hot, suffering cramps and thirst. A rest to admire the view was called for, the prospect over Haweswater being savoured. The summits of Mardale Ill Bell and Harter had not revealed anything of Blea Water or Small Water but subsequent visits rectified this, although I recall a partial view of Small Water from the col at Nan Bield. Examination of the glorious tangle of stones and disused metal fence posts and tighteners which made up the summit cairn was followed by a very necessary intake of fluid plus a little salt via a sandwich.

After about half an hour's break I continued the round, now heading south with the sun becoming ever more hot. Further cramp attacks occurred on the way to Kentmere Pike and it was obvious that I was becoming badly dehydrated. I finished what little fluid remained and pressed on, knowing that if I stopped I would lock up completely. It was at about this point that I was passed by a walker also heading south and he was kind enough to ask if I was o.k. Obviously my discomfort showed but I confirmed an attack of leg cramp and that I would survive, experience having taught me that the best thing to do with cramp is continue if you can! My enquirer continued on his way, but to this day I believe that it was none other than Geoffrey Berry who spoke to me.

The remainder of the round was uneventful with the Ordnance Survey column on the Pike being passed on the way to Shipman Knotts, also passing Goat Scar where I would normally have spent a little more time, but not today! The path eventually met the Kentmere to Sadgill track and my round was completed with the short distance to Kentmere. By then my legs had "gone", and I was extremely dehydrated, although eventual cafe refreshment gave adequate compensation.

It also transpired that it was to prove to be the hottest day of the year. From July onwards it hardly seemed to stop raining until the end of September. St. Swithin lived up to his reputation that year. It had been an unforgettable day, one in which I had learned much, and which remains vivid in my memory.

6. *Skiddaw*

Ullock Pike ridge from Skiddaw

There seems to be an attitude amongst a number of fell-walkers, who perhaps like to consider themselves as hard men, that Skiddaw is not worth the effort. It is the tourists' mountain **par excellence** and therefore beneath contempt. This to me is quite ridiculous. For years I had seen this vast bulk of a mountain, especially from the south, and promised myself that one day I would climb it. Later forays into the North Lakes had revealed Skiddaw with the exciting prospect of the Ullock Pike to Carlside ridge and I decided that this would one day be my route. After careful study of Wainwright's "Northern Fells" I felt that it would be best to start at the Ravenstone hotel on the A591 north of Keswick.

A very pleasant autumn morning found me climbing through Dodd wood. This was hard work, a steep climb before the legs were warmed up and no opportunity to walk off the lead in the limbs. Frequent pauses due to the climb and lack of practice found me very warm and laboured at the lower end of the ridge, having passed through heather in its finest purple cloak. The view from the ridge revealed Bassenthwaite Lake, little troubled by the slight breeze and the Bishop of Barf was clearly visible on the west side of the lake. To the north, the Solway Firth and Criffel in Dumfries could be seen plus Binsey, which is of course "just up the road". Wainwright's advice to climb Binsey to view the northern giants Skiddaw and Blencathra from the north had been taken some time before and had clearly revealed the best approach.

Ullock Pike presented a splendid aspect ahead, and steady progress up the winding ridge path brought me to the summit. Extensive views of shy Southerndale now unfolded, plus a magical perspective of the Derwent Fells beyond Keswick and Derwentwater. A reasonably successful attempt was made to identify the more obvious tops, including Grisedale Pike, Causey Pike, Dale Head, Hindscarth and many others. The prospect of a relatively easy saunter along the ridge to Long Side and Carl Side was savoured and began at a gentle pace. The Skiddaw **massif** seemed to grow larger with every step and the early morning cloud-cap had now gone, with the strengthening sun bathing the summit, whilst the few high clouds gave a beautiful dappled effect to the lower valley and flanks of the mountain. Dodd could now be seen clearly, looking very strange with its trees being felled below the top, presenting a "short back and sides" appearance.

A slight diversion from the path to take in the Carlside cairn was the ideal opportunity for a breather. I looked at Skiddaw and the scree slope I would have to climb. It looked very steep indeed, and its eroded state made it a more awkward proposition than scree would have done. However the foreshortened view always makes an approach seem steeper than it actually is, and the usual stops, to admire the view down Southerndale of course, eventually came to an end as I emerged on the summit plateau between the north and south tops. I decided to visit the main north cairn and strolled along the lunar-like top.

As this is **the** tourists' mountain, I knew there would be a wide variety of souls at the summit and I was not mistaken. There was a family from the south of England who seemed to be adhering to the "safety in numbers and noise" theory, young couples, children kicking cans, fell runners out for practice and "Elton John"! I first saw him whilst trying to distance myself from the general mayhem around me. He was, like me, walking alone. His outfit was superb. A homburg-style hat in soft black leather complemented his shades, whilst his black leather jacket plus cowboy fringes gave him his strong resemblance to the entertainer. He turned out to be a pleasant Scots lad who had come over Skiddaw Little Man and we wandered together down to the south top as he was returning to the Gale Road car park and I had decided not to descend via Bakestall and would return by my approach route since I felt this to be a much better option. Unusual perhaps to backtrack but the weather was superb and staying high as long as possible seemed to be the order of the day. My companion, on reaching the south top, asked me how far it was to Helvellyn. I gave him a rough idea and he then proceeded to shake me rigid by saying he would drive down past Thirlmere and climb it from Wythburn church that afternoon!

At this point I decided I would leave Skiddaw Little Man for another day, when Lonscale Fell would be included. So, when we parted company, I dropped down the scree from the south top and arrived at Carl Side col. By this time more people were about and I saw no reason to change my decision to return along the ridge to Ullock Pike although I did briefly consider descending into Southerndale.

The views from the ridge were superlative as the light had changed and now presented a totally different scene to the one observed earlier in the day. Arrival at Ullock Pike was much too soon and descent began. About half way down I passed two men carrying parachutes; they were obviously not fell walkers! Further down I encountered a young couple who were attending to their gear on a level grassy area.

At this point the girl spoke: "Excuse me, are you going down?"

I confirmed I was, wondering what the next comment would be.

"Do you think you could take the dog down for us, to the end of the ridge?"

The dog was in fact a labrador bitch named Jessie with the usual honey-coloured coat. I mumbled something to the effect that I was not going to the end of the ridge but would leave it to head toward

Dodd Wood, and in any case I was a confirmed cat man. She seemed very disappointed.

"We are going to parascend together down the ridge to the Watches and if we leave Jessie here she may fall and injure herself as she gets very excited when we are parascending. Otherwise I will have to take her down myself and return."

Feeling that I had been shamed into it I agreed to take the labrador down to the Watches where the other members of the club were and who knew the dog. I was instructed to call her Jess and was informed that she was responsive and well behaved. Reluctantly, Jessie followed me down after much coaxing and soon her owner was lost from view. Several minutes elapsed, when cries of "Hello" and "Thank you" came from above. As I admired the passing aerial artists they were then seen by Jessie and her mistress called her name. This grave mistake produced paroxysms of delight in Jessie who leapt into the air vainly trying to reach her mistress. When this failed she charged blindly down the ridge in an attempt to catch up, with stones and dust trailing behind her. Eventually Jessie could no longer see the parascenders and slowly began to respond to my rather vain attempts to restore order. A few minutes of steady progress and she could then see the parachutes spread about around the Watches … then she was gone!

As I came down to the point where I intended to leave the ridge I encountered one of the young parachute enthusiasts, who proceeded to tell me about his sport and the pleasure they obtained from it. I could well understand the excitement of viewing the fells from on high and the quiet enjoyment derived from it.

I then returned to the Ravenstone Hotel reflecting on a splendid day when I had at last climbed Skiddaw, encountered "Elton John", seen parascenders, and temporarily became a dog handler.

7. Loughrigg

Loughrigg Tarn from near summit

Of all the wonderful experiences to be had in the mountains of the Lake District, I have found over the years that it has been not necessarily the highest fells that have given the greatest pleasure.

Wainwright himself admitted to a personal favourite in Haystacks, which is less than 2000ft. Fells of moderate elevation provide excellent vantage points for camera work, where the benefit of mid-height offers varying angles that often produce pictures far better than those taken from a summit. In addition, they are full of interest in their own right. Haystacks I have mentioned but Mellbreak also comes to mind, with views of Grasmoor.

There is however a particular favourite of mine, which also happens to be the favourite of many visitors to the Lakes whether they are tourists or seasoned fell-walkers. I refer to none other than Loughrigg. It happens to be located close to the two main tourist centres of Ambleside and Grasmere but happily has not lost any of its inherent charm because of this, plus the fact that its modest height entices those who would not normally climb a fell, to "have a go". It is unlikely that any navigational difficulty will be encountered as the majority of people reach its summit from the splendid path known as Loughrigg Terrace and simply retrace their steps. Others with experience know all too well that this modest fell of just 1,101ft. possesses a somewhat confusing sprawl over a wide area, with many paths, having access from various points around its base. You can certainly lose your way on Loughrigg, if only fleetingly; mist can make matters worse unless you are familiar with the mountain. Nevertheless it remains a mountain top rich in its variety for those prepared to be a little adventurous.

Always when visiting Loughrigg I am reminded of the occasion maybe twenty years ago when my wife and I had been strolling around at the beginning of our holiday, relaxing, enjoying the freedom and getting our fell-legs back into working order. We had been ambling around Silver How and had begun to return to our regular base in Grasmere, this time via Spedding Crag and High Close, and in order to see the lake we picked up the track through Deerbolts Wood, the latter surprisingly not named on the 1:25000 maps of the Ordnance Survey. This track spits you out right at the corner of the wood where it meets the Terrace, providing a "surprise view". Imagine **our** surprise to find ourselves confronted with a scene so out of place in this idyllic little corner that we did a "double take". Before us, at the gate, were a man and woman, both dressed in the most resplendent "Wild-West" clothes you could imagine! Straight from Texas with frills everywhere, a stetson, high-heeled boots, decorative spurs, leather skirt, the lot! After desperately trying to recover our composure quickly, we realized that we had been spotted and the man was heading straight for us. He was looking around as he did so, particularly at the path up to Loughrigg summit.

He spoke: "D'ya know any good walks around here?" he said, in a glorious American-deep-south drawl. Considering our location it seemed a rather fatuous question to ask but conversation ensued wherein he confirmed that yes, they were tourists over from the States and were enjoying their visit and had ventured out for a little exercise.

"It will take about twenty minutes" I said, looking at the path up to the Grasmere cairn, thinking that this was what he had in mind, "but it's a little steep".

He replied, with a deep frown: "It looks **very** steep to me!"

Obviously something had got lost in translation, it being a perfect example of two nations divided by a common language. The upshot was that he decided that the two of them could not possibly climb this huge mountain and they would continue along the Terrace. His parting shot was an absolute gem.

"By the way", he said, "I just lurv your City of Grasmere!"

Stunned, as if in a dream, we made our way back.

*One Fell below 1000 ft...
See page 58*

8. *Steel Fell*

Steel Fell and Helvellyn from Helm Crag ridge

There is no doubt that most of us have our favourite fells. In Wainwright's case he always reckoned it to be the one he happened to be on at the time. Why Steel Fell? I find it very hard to answer, although having thought about it in later years I believe it may have been merely the fact that it was akin to an oasis of quiet compared with its near neighbour Helm Crag, which seems to have many visitors irrespective of the time of year.

As we spent many of our holidays based in Grasmere it was only logical that the Central Fells would be visited more frequently than those in parts of the Lakes with more difficult access. It also meant that on arrival it was almost standard practice to undertake a leg-stretch, and the route that always seemed to fit the bill for me was that of the Helm Crag ridge as far as the isolated stile near Calf Crag, then turning to follow the fence along the top of Steel Fell to the two tarns culminating in the view from the summit north to Thirlmere and Blencathra. On one or two occasions this excursion was done in reverse, but I invariably found the southeast ridge hard work, especially if the round was undertaken on a hot summer's day, when there was no escape from the sun.

Subsequent visits to the area revealed the shy Greenburn Valley. It became eventually the only way to complete a round where Steel Fell was the main objective. Not only was it less busy than the Helm Crag ridge but there was also an almost tangible air of mystery about Greenburn, probably due to the drumlins at the valley head being visible proof of the last Ice age, which eventually became part of a popular short walk usually undertaken anti-clockwise starting from Gill Foot along Green Burn toward Greenburn Bottom, striking up onto the Helm Crag ridge leaving the stroll southeastwards along the ridge with Grasmere and its lake always ahead for appreciation. When heading for Steel Fell the ridge was traversed westwards to Calf Crag and Brownrigg Moss to meet our friendly stile again.

Occasionally variations were undertaken such as striking along the valley floor of Far Easedale as far as the aforementioned stile, which was invariably climbed in a nonsensical ritual, but fun nevertheless, at Brownrigg Moss. The walk northeastwards on Steel Fell was always undertaken at a leisurely pace to savour the traverse, usually halting at the unnamed tarns for an appreciation of the crags on the southeast flank of Ullscarf, itself a brooding, moody moonscape of a fell especially in misty conditions. In later years these tarns were to provide much-needed coolant for overheated bodies!

Following the stop to appreciate the view the short pull up to the summit of the fell was rewarded with splendid views northwards through Dunmail to Thirlmere with Blencathra's southern aspect for the backdrop. The descent, on first acquaintance, was to provide unexpected splendid snapshots of the Helvellyn ridge across Dunmail especially when negotiating the Ash Crags area.

This simple unassuming fell does not have the grandeur of the Scafells or the Wasdale giants, but in the subjective nature of favourites this particular area is for me highly atmospheric and peaceful, and as such will always evoke fond memories. Other more well-known fells may be higher and have more obvious attributes but this relatively little known fell will hold a special place in my affections, having been climbed at all times of the year.

9. Sergeant Man

Easedale Tarn from Blea Rigg ridge approaching Sergeant Man

In my earlier years in the Lakeland hills during visits to our central base in Grasmere, one of the focal points on the fells beyond Easedale was a prominent cairn. Sentinel-like, it drew the eye unerringly to it whenever the far hills were observed. It became so prominent that it obviously had to be visited. Careful study of the map revealed that this was in fact Sergeant Man.

I remember the initial ascent was made via Easedale Tarn, passing Belles Knot onto the Blea Rigg ridge. It was inevitably boggy this way so other routes were explored. Trying Codale Tarn was obviously no better as the bog between Easedale Tarn and Eagle Crag had still to be traversed, although Codale was a pleasantly quiet, albeit rather haunting, place. Eventually I decided that the best way for me was to leave Grasmere by the track alongside the "Coffee Bean", passing Allan Bank on the way to Lang How, bypassing Silver How, to pick up the Blea Rigg ridge, passing the tarns generally known as Seagull Tarns. Another way onto this ridge was to go to Easedale Tarn and then strike southwest past the side of Blea Crag. Either way was better than the boggy route. Return could be made by the route not used on approach although a far better and quieter way was via Tarn Crag, returning to Grasmere via Far Easedale. These options were used many times over the years and were always pleasurable. In later years the summit cairn was vandalised, removing a splendid spire from the skyline. Indeed this summit became a particular favourite, being always involved whenever walks were undertaken in the area, including the Langdale Pikes. Walks would be made through to Greenup Edge from Grasmere via Far Easedale and then south to High Raise. Continuation to Sergeant Man then gave options of returning to Grasmere via either Tarn Crag or the Blea Rigg ridge, with an occasional variation down to Easedale Tarn.

It was whilst in this area one day that I encountered two ladies who by the nature of their dress and bearing seemed to be seasoned fell-walkers. At the time I was fairly new to this wonderful pursuit and after entering into conversation was immediately admonished for looking around whilst moving and not looking where I was putting my feet! Shades of Wainwright here! We were in the vicinity of Tarn Crag and they had arrived on a bus from Carnforth, and were undertaking a round to a timetable in order to catch the last bus back from Grasmere. So the pace was quite high and soon one of the ladies and I were falling behind the leader, who was dressed in an appropriately fashioned headscarf and long flowing tweed skirt. She was fairly flying! After much grumbling about the pace and chatting to my companion it transpired that our leader was highly experienced and whom I also learnt was seventy-two years old! "Oh yes", said my companion, "she also bought her first ice-axe when she was seventy!"

As I was not under any time pressure, our ways eventually parted and I continued my wanderings, eventually arriving back in Grasmere about teatime. Passing near the bus stop at Parrock Green, who should I see but the two ladies waiting for their return transport.

I often think of them whenever in Grasmere and wonder whether the ice-axe was ever put to serious use.

10. Great Gable

Great Gable from Kirk Fell

Great Gable is a name of which many people have heard, even those who would never even contemplate setting foot on a mountain. For many Lakeland fell-walkers however it is **the** one above all others. It is not the highest but its part in the creation of Lakes folklore cannot be underestimated. The romance of the early climbers, whose interest was only in achieving ever-harder climbs rather than summits, is mooted in the Wasdale Inn at the foot of Gable.

It was however some years after reading the print off Wainwright's book seven that the opportunity arrived to venture onto hallowed ground.

Being on holiday near Windermere with the weather forecast set fair, I duly rose very early and travelled to Honister Hause arriving at about 7 a.m. My route would be via the Drum House, then heading south to Grey Knotts, Brandreth and Green Gable and onto the summit from Windy Gap. It cannot have escaped the reader's notice that I had saved about 1000ft. of climbing by choosing this route!

And so it was that I left the car park by the quarry buildings and trekked up the old tramway to the Drum House. Rather than pick up Moses' Trod at the Brandreth fence I had already decided that I would walk over the summits on the way to Gable. The day was perfect with birds in full song, particularly the skylarks, and there was no one else around. The walking was magical. On arrival at the summit of Grey Knotts time was spent exploring the tarns although they were quite small and then the fence was followed to Brandreth. This wander was being conducted at a leisurely pace; such was the pleasure of the moment. Even though it was early in the day I was wearing sunglasses and had lapsed into the lone walker's habit, {mine certainly!}, of talking to oneself. On towards Green Gable on the short drop to the col with sunglasses to the fore I suddenly found myself confronted by a tent, with its occupant outside cooking eggs and bacon. What he made of me I know not and he did not press my obvious embarrassment. He did however offer me a "buttie" as he could plainly see I was salivating not having had breakfast, and such a treat **al fresco** early in the day was sheer bliss. Thanking my benefactor I hauled myself up the climb to Green Gable where I rested awhile until my thoughts were rudely interrupted by a couple of men who seemed rather agitated.

"Is this the way to Scafell?" one of them enquired. Now no doubt there are fell-walkers who choose to visit the Scafells via Gable but these two did not appear to have any maps nor was their equipment particularly reassuring. They were also unclear as to their route, not being sure whether they wanted Scafell or Scafell Pike. As they were obviously very keen to press on regardless I felt that the best thing to do was to suggest that they reconsider their options once they reached the summit of Gable, having done a bit of climbing to get there, when they may then be a little more aware of what was involved. Off they went and I did not see them again. My own ascent to the summit was achieved without further encounters, and I spent some time looking at the First World War Memorial on the summit. I then sat at the Westmorland Cairn and enjoyed the view of Wasdale although the mist was capricious and rendered the taking of photographs rather difficult. Returning to the summit, yet again my quiet contemplation was rudely interrupted. A very noisy group of young men numbering about six was "smashing" its way towards the summit. On arrival there, their leader espoused: "This is worrit's all about." Presumably he meant reaching the summit but as the group stayed not more than a few minutes I was not sure this was so. Eventually the group disappeared eastwards so I assumed Sty Head was the destination. Obviously I was not destined to have a quiet day so I decided to return. The possibility of a visit to Base Brown was considered but on arrival at the decision point of Green Gable decided to leave that for another day.

All in all a fascinating day, where three separate scenarios had encapsulated the variety of people and attitudes encountered on the fells. For me only one of these really knew "worrit's all about" and he was alone, enjoying his bacon and eggs whilst contemplating the day ahead.

*27 Fells 1001 ft. to 1500 ft...
see page 59*

11. Mosedale

Steeple

After some years fell-walking it was becoming obvious that there were certain rounds that were held in very high esteem among walkers, and as I began to achieve more summits it was apparent that I would eventually have to tackle a number of reputedly very tough rounds, which had been quietly ignored in the hope that they might go away! Among these was the Mosedale Horseshoe. I had read of it many times over a number of years but the likelihood of ever getting to grips with it seemed remote.

A very pleasant late summer day some years ago found me at Wasdale Head, early, to tackle this famed circuit. I had decided to be sensible and not attempt the purists' round, which would have included Kirk Fell and Yewbarrow, reasoning that there was to be enough sweat ahead without crucifying myself and perhaps creating unnecessary difficulties.

An earlier reconnaissance had taken in Mosedale when I had crossed the bridge behind the Wasdale Head Inn and explored the valley along Mosedale Beck. This time it was to be for real as I headed for the Black Sail Pass. A steady ascent found me alongside Gatherstone Beck, without any problems, and eventual arrival at the col between Pillar and Kirk Fell, the Black Sail Pass, at about 1800ft. The seemingly insignificant Looking Stead proved to be a little more awkward than anticipated, having chosen to go via its highest point at about 2000ft. rather than the more usual track. It was here that I had wild delusions of achieving the summit of Pillar via the High Level Route and the Robinson Cairn. After some minutes agonizing I decided to stick to my original plan, leaving that route for another day.

The remaining 800ft. to the summit of Pillar was accomplished without difficulty, following the line of the ruined fence. And so after many years of contemplation, here I was on top of one of the most famous mountains in the Lake District. Was it what I had anticipated? Hard to say except that it was most definitely very stony and moon-like, thoroughly deserving its nickname: "The Bald Mountain". Pillar Rock I did not even contemplate!

Leaving the trig. point in a southwesterly direction found me heading for Black Crag via the Wind Gap col on my way to Scoat Fell to resolve the mystery of the Scoats, Little and Great. The summit cairn, which is in fact on top of a wall, is also on Little Scoat Fell, with "Little" referring only to the area of the fell rather than its stature. Great Scoat Fell is of much larger area but not as high. Deciding not to be totally stupid I decided against climbing the wall to touch the topmost point of the cairn and proceeded to the one at the start of the descent onto the path to Steeple.

This is a must for any self-respecting fell-walker, being an airy one-quarter-mile walk to the summit, where, if the day is clear, a wonderful sense of space is encountered from its very small summit area; but it is definitely not the place for an afternoon nap with crags beneath your feet.

With time pressing, a regretful retracing of steps was necessary to the cairn on Scoat, before moving across an awkward area of small boulders on the way to the summit of Red Pike, losing a little height down into the dip before rising to the splendid cairn which is situated on the very edge of the escarpment where, yet again, by standing right at the cairn a tremendous sense of space is enjoyed overlooking the whole of Mosedale. It had been my intention to look for "The Chair" on the way to Dore Head but as I was beginning to tire I completely forgot about it; remembering, I did not feel like retracing my steps **upwards** once again! After negotiating Gosforth Crag, nothing really, but irksome to aching legs, I eventually arrived at Dore Head.

Decision time! Dore Head is perhaps now as infamous as it once was famous. Nowadays it is little more than a mudslide, whereas generations ago walkers were able to enjoy a grand scree slope. The scree is now all at the foot of the slope in Mosedale. My arrival at Dore Head coincided with that of four other walkers who had been on the same route as myself since Scoat Fell, maintaining similar progress.

After some discussion, it was agreed that to climb Yewbarrow or follow Over Beck down to the road and then round to Wasdale was at this time a bit too much to undertake so Dore Head it was to be. We all began our descent into Mosedale, initially in-line but soon fanning out across the slope after a couple of near misses for the leaders from small rocks disturbed by the last members of the party. Make no mistake; this is a seemingly endless slope for tired legs. It is also unremittingly steep. About halfway down my old adversary cramp set in with a vengeance, as usual choosing a situation where I was unable to give my legs any respite. There was nothing for it but to continue, and try and walk through it. Progress was now very slow indeed and my erstwhile companions had reached the foot of the slope and had begun to wander along the valley floor towards Wasdale, whilst I was still coming down ever so slowly towards the scree at the bottom. Eventually I arrived, coming through the scree with legs not responding to my wishes, trying to carefully negotiate the bracken to avoid ticks on my legs. Not recommended at that time of the year!

Now I too was able to make my way towards Wasdale. It had been my intention to have a close look at Ritson's Force but even this was too much and I contented myself with a distant view.

I had completed a wonderful, if tough, walk, which is as fresh in my memory now as when I undertook it. It is certainly one of Lakeland's gems.

*59 Fells 1501 ft. to 2000 ft...
see pages 60 - 62 inc.*

12. Scafell Pike

Trig. Point, Scafell Pike summit

Over the years Scafell Pike had begun to haunt me. Not only was it the highest mountain in England but also relatively inaccessible. Most of our time in the Lakes was spent based at Grasmere, so to even contemplate the climbing of Scafell Pike would involve a time consuming trip to Wasdale and consequently was put on the back-burner.

When the time came to confront the issue we had acquired another base in the North Lakes between Cockermouth and Carlisle. This locale still made for an equally long trip, so for the occasion my son Mark decided to accompany me. He had never been on a fell before, and has not been on one since. He merely wished to be able to say that he had climbed the highest mountain in England!

And so a very early start was made. I had decided to start from Borrowdale on the basis that it would probably be a once and only event and had chosen what I perceived to be the most interesting route. The weather was fortunately quite clement and we were able to concentrate solely on the business of upward propulsion. Leaving Seathwaite good progress was made and soon Stockley Bridge was behind us and Sty Head lay ahead. Onto familiar territory at Esk Hause through Calf Cove and the track to Great End, which I had visited some months earlier in thick mist during which I met a couple who were on their first trip out following the wife's operation for a hip replacement. A further trip up Kilimanjaro was planned for later in the year! Our trip was perhaps far less glamourous but nevertheless every bit as important to us: the matter of relativity again.

We then encountered the rather awkward boulder field reached before Ill Crag, this being about 200yds. long. My perambulation was à la Wainwright in such situations i.e. inelegant. Meanwhile Mark was boulder-hopping despite my warnings about broken ankles and was making good progress, then patiently waiting for me to catch up. Eventually this travail reached an end and having lost height down to the Ill Crag col climbed up Broad Crag to see yet another downward slope to the Broad Crag col. At last the final slope onto the Pike was achieved and with the knowledge that there were no more false summits to come, was reached quite quickly. Time was spent on the summit taking photographs, which is of course **de rigueur**, before continuing our journey.

As our return was via the Corridor Route this meant a drop to the Lingmell col, so it was decided to take in the summit of Lingmell **en route**. My first cramps of the day occurred on the climb but were walked through. The views of Gable from Lingmell were tremendous, quite the best I feel; better than from Kirk Fell.

On now past the end of Piers Gill with all its historical horror stories but pausing long enough to wonder at the forces of nature that created it, we continued past Greta Gill onto Skew Gill, eventually arriving at the stretcher box at Sty Head. Perhaps if we had chosen to ascend in the opposite direction Mark may have been fazed by the sight of such equipment early in the trip, which serves as a constant reminder not to take these old hills lightly.

Again we spent time absorbing our surroundings. Sty Head has always been a personal favourite of mine so it was good to relax there. Remembering to cross Styhead Gill at the bridge, as I really didn't want to scramble across Taylor Gill with tired legs, we arrived at Stockley Bridge.

Our journey was done. The Pike was in the bag at last! Weary yes, but elated certainly.

It then occurred to me that Mark had been wearing gloves throughout and as it was quite warm I enquired as to the reason. He replied: "You remember your trip up Grisedale Pike?"

More on this follows!

71 Fells 2001 ft. to 2500 ft…
see pages 63 – 65 inc.

13. Grisedale Pike

The author on stormy Grisedale Pike

Grisedale Pike. This is a name that I am unlikely to forget whenever the fells are discussed. It is visible from Keswick with the main path an eroded scar. It is also memorable in being one of the rare occasions on which I was accompanied on my walk. My companion had been to the Lakes before and had climbed Scafell Pike, albeit some years ago, and consequently was somewhat out of practice.

The day began with the usual early start. This to me has always been important. Plenty of time in hand is always preferable to being under pressure and this day was to prove the sense in that philosophy. It was in fact a typical August day. It had been unsettled, i.e. wet and warm, for several days. At valley level it was very humid, consequently the wish to travel light was tempered by the necessity to transport the usual wet gear in the rucksack, which meant we were going to have a very hot and sticky climb. As it was so warm my companion had decided to wear jeans and a light top although I made a comment in passing regarding unsuitability.

We were to do the climb from Braithwaite and duly parked at the gravel pit on the Whinlatter road. Early signs confirmed initial fears; it was going to be a very sticky and uncomfortable day. Initial progress was good and some relief from the initial ascent was found when we arrived at Kinn, where we enjoyed a relative stroll at 1100ft. Eventually we began to climb again and Sleet How was gained at about the 1800ft. contour. It was at this juncture that we noted the weather had taken a turn for the worse in complete contrast to that at valley level. The wind had increased noticeably now that we were on an exposed ridge and it had also begun to rain. Carrying on towards the summit we had not only to fight the now very cold wind but also driving rain which was making upward progress very difficult on the wet, slippery path. Indeed it was impossible to stay upright and a crouching, scrambling mode was adopted. Eventually we arrived at the summit where the wind and rain increased markedly in intensity. By this time I had donned my wet gear and my companion his top. Photographs were taken hurriedly as the rain was heavy and almost horizontal, the wind very strong, the temperature very cold. In fact it was classic hypothermia weather and it was now that my companion began to feel cold and started to shiver but had nothing extra to wear. The obvious recourse was therefore to get off the mountain as quickly as possible.

The descent by the same route commenced and immediately we were confronted with stones, which had been present over the last few hundred feet of our ascent. Normally these would have been of no real account, being something that is encountered on most fell-walks and accepted as the norm. This day however was rather different. Everywhere was wet, the rain heavy, the wind strong, the temperature cold. We were descending and most importantly we were moving much too quickly as my companion was by now very cold and wished to lose height as rapidly as possible to get down to more amenable conditions. He was ahead of me as I was trying to negotiate slippery rocks carefully, but even so we were going too quickly. I slipped and slammed my left hand down to stop myself sliding down further. It was then that I noticed that the heel of my hand had opened up. I had smacked a rock very hard when sliding. The wound was very nasty and it was obvious that medical attention would be necessary as soon as possible. My initial reaction was one of shock coupled with rising panic. The wound was strapped up with a handkerchief, which was the best we could do. The situation was discussed and it was evident we could make our way down carefully albeit much more slowly. It was at that time that I appreciated the automatic balance of the human body, for having only three effective limbs meant I needed to compensate and I found this to be extremely difficult, plus the fact that the last thing I needed was another fall. The incident had occurred in the Sleet How area so the easier terrain along Kinn lay ahead. My companion meanwhile was still cold, wishing to descend quickly, but feeling he must accompany me down. Slow progress was made but fortunately as we lost height the weather began to improve and it was not overlong before we were nearing the gravel pit and our transport.

Two more things then became apparent. Firstly my watch had gone, obviously ripped from my wrist in the fall and secondly my companion could not stand the sight of blood! Further consultation resulted in the decision to visit Keswick Cottage Hospital, which was not too far away. Without dwelling overmuch, suffice to say my hand had opened up revealing the tendons. Extensive cleaning, antibiotics, tetanus injection, new dressings every three days, strapped up and no driving for a month. How perverse that I had my mishap adjacent to Hospital Plantation!

It has been pointed out to me that this incident illustrated the benefit of having a companion on the fells. My answer is that it is highly likely that it would not have happened had I been alone.

Perhaps the reader will now understand the reason why my son Mark wore gloves during our ascent of Scafell Pike!

52 Fells 2501 ft. to 3000 ft...
see pages 66 –67 inc.

14. Binsey

John and Eileen on Binsey with Meg and Ben, who were enjoying being chauffeured

In the early 1990s there emerged another fell which was beginning to make itself more and more prominent in the unclimbed stakes. Whilst the likes of Bannerdale Crags and Skiddaw etc. had been explored, the lesser heights had been left for later when time permitted. Among these was Binsey, considered to be little more than a pudding that had to be climbed in order to achieve the 214 Wainwright summits.

Whilst staying with friends in the Wigton area the decision was taken to venture onto Binsey on the following day. It was winter and the weather was fine and dry, but we were in for quite a surprise the following morning when a substantial snowfall had arrived overnight and therefore it would be necessary to add an extra warm layer of clothing for the trip.

The start point was to be Binsey Lodge and we duly arrived there to a very wintry scene. The top of Binsey could not be seen, being shrouded in a dense mist above the 1300ft. level. I should at this point mention that our two friends, John and Eileen, had recently acquired two Jack Russell terriers, Meg and Ben and this would be their introduction to snow as well as their first attempt at walking in it. From the Lodge it is only about a mile to the summit but it soon became fairly evident that the dogs were struggling with the snow. Their legs were shorter than the depth of it and they sank up to their chests with each step and struggled to heave themselves out to make the next one. This was really a classic case for dog snowshoes! Meanwhile the mist was thickening and creeping down the fell. As well as the dogs we also were finding the going awkward and often were up to our knees in small drifts. However we were not to be daunted. Whoever heard of anyone abandoning an ascent of Binsey? We were now in the murk and whilst we could not see the summit all we needed to do was keep heading upwards and soon enough we would arrive. However the dogs were by now exhausted. Therefore John and Eileen each took a dog and Meg and Ben were placed into a bag and rucksack respectively. Whilst looking far from happy to begin with, being rather cold and tired, they then soon began to realise that this was indeed the best way to travel and visibly brightened once they became aware that they would not have to walk any more that day!

Eventually we all arrived at the top of Binsey, still in mist, after what had seemed a much longer distance than a mile. Almost on cue whilst coffee was being drunk, the mist began to lift and within a few minutes the sun was shining, so strongly in fact that sunglasses would have been very useful against the glare from the snow. Alas only one of our party was so equipped as we did not expect to see any sun that day, which only goes to prove that you have to be equipped for all weathers in the Lakes irrespective of the time of year. The fact that there is an ancient tumulus on Binsey elicited little comment other than being noted. The view south however was very impressive, with Skiddaw and Blencathra clothed in a white mantle and it was very interesting to see them from a totally different aspect.

As carrying dogs is not usually part of fell-walking, the extra effort was being felt even on a benign lump like Binsey, and it was decided to return by our approach route, which again is a fairly rare occurrence but understandable in the circumstances. Having picked out Over Water, illuminated brightly by the sun and indeed a shining level, we headed towards it and eventually arrived at the Lodge again, having been able to enjoy a magnificent aspect that had been presented to us by the magical combination of sun and snow.

A very minor expedition that far outweighed our expectations for such a modest fell.

4 Fells over 3000 ft.
see page 68

15. Caw Fell

Caw Fell

There is not a lot that one can say about Caw Fell. Its significance for me is nothing more than the fact that it was my last of Wainwright's 214 summits. Indeed it should have been visited when I climbed Haycock but that particular trip, which was undertaken from Netherbeck Bridge, Wasdale, was one of those days when I was not in the best form and the short distance to Caw Fell was just too much at the time. I later regretted that decision because I had let myself in for another long day when half an hour would have seen me out and back to Caw Fell from Haycock.

So that was the reason that I eventually found myself at Bowness Point, having decided that another visit to shy Ennerdale would be undertaken to finish off the last summit with a pleasant, quiet day, albeit a round trip of approximately ten miles; in the event so it proved. Once the walk down the valley to Low Gillerthwaite was done, there remained the ascent, which was better once the open fellside was reached and only then did it become apparent that this was indeed a relatively unknown back door route to Pillar and Haycock rather than the more well known Wasdale avenues. How pleasant it was to walk on a fell-side that hadn't been turned into a river of stones; indeed walking on grass for the latter part of the climb was a great pleasure. On reaching the ridge I decided to postpone the main reason for the climb, and paid a visit to Little Gowder Crag. I then followed the wall to the summit of Caw Fell.

Mission accomplished! It is very hard to describe one's feelings at such a moment having striven for this finale for several years. Suffice to say quiet satisfaction would be an understatement. Photographs were duly taken although there was very little to capture apart from the summit cairn. I have many photos of piles of stones taken in the Lakes!

Unusually this trip also meant a return by the route of ascent. During this time my thoughts strayed to other cameos, among many, which have not been recorded in detail in this book. The occasion when I had toothache and ventured onto Place Fell heading to Sleet Fell and Howtown and along the way met a **dentist**; the time on Helm Crag when I met a lady who admitted she was new to the pursuit of fell-walking and was finding it "a little scary at times" but was beginning to really enjoy it. She had been widowed for only a few months so had decided to see what it was that had interested her late husband for so many years; the magnificent day to Scafell over Slight Side from Wha House, Eskdale returning via Cam Spout to Lingcove Bridge; the amazing Bakestones missed by many on the Fairfield Horseshoe. Countless other images would have presented themselves but my reverie was interrupted by the totally unexpected sight of another human being, the first I had seen since leaving Bowness Point where there had been a crowd of two. The camaraderie of the fells is always to the fore and this encounter was no different. We chatted for a while and I simply had to tell the young walker that I was in fact descending from Caw Fell having just achieved my final Wainwright.

"Congratulations!" he said. "It's a great experience isn't it? I've already done them all once. Now I'm doing them again!"

So the great adventure came to its end. I would not have missed it for anything.

To those readers who may feel it is a daunting prospect I would say do it.

You will need something to tell your grandchildren.

*

Alfred Wainwright later produced a Book 8, "The Outlying Fells", wherein he records a total of 102 less well-known fells.

But that, perhaps, may be another story …

The following pages list the heights of all 214 summits in ascending order.

The only fell listed below 1,000 ft. is

Castle Crag   985 ft.

27 Fells 1001 ft. to 1500 ft.

Holme Fell	1040
Black Fell	1056
Loughrigg Fell	1101
Rannerdale Knotts	1160
High Rigg	1163
Sale Fell	1170
Troutbeck Tongue	1191
Latrigg	1203
Ling Fell	1224
Walla Crag	1234
Hallin Fell	1271
Silver How	1292
Helm Crag	1299
Low Fell	1360
Fellbarrow	1363
Grange Fell	1363
Gibson Knott	1379
Buckbarrow	1410
Steel Knotts	1414
Arnison Crag	1424
Glenridding Dodd	1425
Nab Scar	1450
Binsey	1466
Graystones	1476
Catbells	1481
Barrow	1494
Great Crag	1500

59 Fells 1501 ft. to 2000 ft.

Raven Crag	1520
Lingmoor Fell	1530
Barf	1536
Sour Howes	1568
Armboth Fell	1570
Gowbarrow Fell	1579
Burnbank Fell	1580
Longlands Fell	1580
Grike	1596
Wansfell	1597
Green Crag	1602
Dodd	1612
Eagle Crag	1650
Stone Arthur	1652
Low Pike	1657
Little Mell Fell	1657
Hen Comb	1661
Beda Fell	1664
High Tove	1665
Broom Fell	1670
Mellbreak	1676
Souther Fell	1680
Sallows	1691
Whinlatter	1696
High Hartsop Dodd	1702
Crag Fell	1710
Bonscale Pike	1718

59 Fells 1501 ft. to 2000 ft.
(continued)

Gavel Fell	1720
Great Cockup	1720
Arthur's Pike	1747
Whin Rigg	1755
Great Mell Fell	1760
Calf Crag	1762
Meal Fell	1770
Lank Rigg	1775
Blea Rigg	1776
Knott Rigg	1790
Tarn Crag (Easedale)	1801
Hard Knott	1803
Rosthwaite Fell	1807
Lord's Seat	1811
Steel Fell	1811
Brock Crags	1842
Angletarn Pikes	1857
Ard Crags	1860
Outerside	1863
Hartsop Above How	1870
Sergeant's Crag	1873
Blake Fell	1878
Maiden Moor	1887
The Nab	1887
Haystacks	1900
Middle Fell	1908

59 Fells 1501 ft. to 2000 ft.
(continued)

Brae Fell	1920
Shipman Knotts	1926
Bleaberry Fell	1932
Seathwaite Fell	1970
Illgill Head	1983
High Seat	1995

71 Fells 2001 ft. to 2500 ft.

Heron Pike	2003
Hartsop Dodd	2018
Great Borne	2019
Causey Pike	2035
Birks	2040
Yewbarrow	2058
Mungrisdale Common	2068
Starling Dodd	2085
Little Hart Crag	2091
Grey Crag	2093
Middle Dodd	2106
Rossett Pike	2106
Base Brown	2120
Fleetwith Pike	2126
Great Sca Fell	2131
Harter Fell (Eskdale)	2140
Selside Pike	2142
High Spy	2143
Place Fell	2154
High Pike (Scandale)	2155
High Pike (Caldbeck)	2157
Whiteless Pike	2159
Carrock Fell	2174
Tarn Crag (Longsleddale)	2176
Bakestall	2189
Loadpot Hill	2201
Scar Crags	2205

71 Fells 2001 ft. to 2500 ft.
(continued)

Wether Hill	2210
Bannerdale Crags	2230
Ullock Pike	2230
Sheffield Pike	2232
Cold Pike	2259
Great Calva	2265
Seatallan	2266
Loft Crag	2270
Rest Dodd	2278
Gray Crag	2286
Grey Knotts	2287
Caw Fell	2288
Pavey Ark	2288
Pike o' Blisco	2304
Bowscale Fell	2306
Yoke	2309
Whiteside	2317
Pike o' Stickle	2323
Knott	2329
Branstree	2333
Brandreth	2344
Lonscale Fell	2344
Birkhouse Moor	2350
Thunacar Knott	2351
Froswick	2359
Ullscarf	2370

71 Fells 2001 ft. to 2500 ft.
(continued)

Clough Head	2381
Hindscarth	2385
Kentmere Pike	2397
Harrison Stickle	2403
Long Side	2405
Sergeant Man	2414
Seat Sandal	2415
Robinson	2417
Carl Side	2420
The Knott	2423
High Crag	2443
Dale Head	2473
Ill Bell	2476
Red Pike (Buttermere)	2479
Hart Side	2481
Mardale Ill Bell	2496
Slightside	2499
High Raise (Langdale)	2500

52 Fells 2501 ft. to 3000 ft.

Caudale Moor	2502
Wetherlam	2502
Great Rigg	2513
Hopegill Head	2525
Sail	2530
Wandope	2533
Grey Friar	2536
Harter Fell (Mardale)	2539
Red Screes	2541
Dow Crag	2555
Glaramara	2560
Kidsty Pike	2560
Thornthwaite Crag	2569
Allen Crags	2572
Great Carrs	2575
Rampsgill Head	2581
Watson's Dodd	2584
Grisedale Pike	2593
Dove Crag	2603
Green Gable	2603
Brim Fell	2611
Haycock	2618
Kirk Fell	2630
Swirl How	2630
Coniston Old Man	2633
High Raise (Martindale)	2634
High Stile	2644

52 Fells 2501 ft. to 3000 ft.
(continued)

Lingmell	2649
Steeple	2687
Hart Crag	2698
Red Pike (Wasdale)	2707
High Street	2718
Eel Crag	2749
Saint Sunday Crag	2756
Scoat Fell	2760
Stybarrow Dodd	2770
Grasmoor	2791
Great Dodd	2807
Dollywaggon Pike	2810
Crinkle Crags	2816
Whiteside	2832
Skiddaw Little Man	2837
Blencathra	2847
Fairfield	2863
Raise	2889
Esk Pike	2903
Catstycam	2917
Nethermost Pike	2920
Pillar	2927
Great Gable	2949
Bowfell	2960
Great End	2984

4 Fells over 3000 ft.

Skiddaw	3053
Helvellyn	3118
Scafell	3162
Scafell Pike	3210